The Fight To Find An Answer

How To Get Help For A Loved One With Dementia

V.V. Marie, & Rhys Shaw

Pens Of Three Publishing

Have you ever thought a loved one may be showing signs of dementia? Are you scared to find out? Or are you having a difficult time getting help or answers?

The authors wrote this book because they have traveled this road with their loved ones. They aren't medical professionals, but they want you to know what they have gone through to fight for a diagnosis. It wasn't easy for them, but hopefully, reading this book will give you some guidance in your situation and assist you in taking action.

This book shares the struggles and experiences of several families, regarding how difficult it was to get a diagnosis and, finally, help for a family member suffering from dementia.

Inside, you will also find early warning signs, conversation starters to go over with your primary care provider to help rule out other reasons for your concerns, next steps/questions to go over with your care provider if the symptoms persist, tasks you can take care of before you get a diagnosis, tips on how to advocate for additional needs, additional sources to get help, and tips on how to interview for a care facility if needed.

Book Cover by Livinia Penn

First edition 2026 ISBN 978-1-970758-01-6

Contents

Introduction

We are not doctors, nor are we professionals specializing in dementia. We are just daughters who, when the signs were there, wanted to get the help for our mothers. We realized there was a flood of information for the disease, like so much is in this day and age, and we didn't know where to start. It's hard to tell who was just out to sell crap, who actually cared, and who was legit. And most importantly, we didn't understand why our mothers' doctors wouldn't take our concerns seriously. This book wouldn't even have needed to be written if we hadn't noticed this frustrating pattern to find information is far too common.

This book is not meant to be used as medical advice or to replace any medical advice given by medical professionals. The opinions offered are just that: opinions from people with no claim to medical knowledge, just experience in life.

What this book isn't. If you are looking for a full comprehensive academic article on dementia, this isn't it. If you picked this book up to find some nefarious tactics to acquire someone's assets, you won't get it here—leave now and go find a conscience.

What this book is. If you are led to believe you or someone you love is starting to show signs of dementia or you aren't even sure and are scared to make the wrong decision, this book will help guide you to action. Like many who are worried about a disease, you go to your primary care physician to express concerns, and if nothing comes of it, you're similar to the people in this book. Whether they disregarded your concerns or complimented you on how well you or the loved one is doing for "their age." You feel gaslit into believing all is well, as your medical professional should know best. Or your loved one is decent enough in using subterfuge and hides it from all except those who are most often with them. (Chances are they aren't doing this out of malicious intent, but they are frightened of the diagnosis and what that could mean for them or they may not even know they're doing it, as it's turned into a common crutch response.) You may recognize your concerns are being overlooked and don't know where to go. This book will help you possibly find the courage to pursue a provider who will listen, some resources to help, typical early warning signs, activities anyone can do to help decelerate the situation, additional sources to get help in the interim to finding a provider, a few starting points on getting help after you've gotten the diagnosis, and some tips on what to look for in a care facility if it's needed.

In this book, you'll hear from several different people who have experienced the disheartening task of trying to get a diagnosis or to even find an answer. This way you can see what others went through and use the knowledge of their experiences to your advantage. Especially if you are going through something similar, it better shows the roadblocks and ways to traverse them.

If you don't have a lot of time to read a twenty-thousand-plus word book because you don't need to hear other people's stories, or someone prattling on about dementia, and you want to get to the meat and potatoes of the work, I understand. So in short:

- Keep advocating.

- Find a new doctor and another new doctor until you come across someone who is willing to listen to your concerns, or send you to a neurologist where you can finally get the treatment you need.

- The titles of each chapter are set up to let you get to whatever you are looking for, jump to what you need to get to. The chapter "Helpful Resources" is not a comprehensive list for links, resources, or ideas to help, and I'm sure there are more out there that are equally useful, but these are the ones we, friends, or professionals have suggested or used and can be used as a springboard.

Now that that's all out of the way, onto the rest of the book.

Dementia in Short

The *Encyclopedia Britannica*'s definition of dementia is a "general term for any of a number of conditions marked by chronic, usually progressive deterioration of intellectual capacity associated with the widespread loss of nerve cells and the shrinkage of brain tissue. People with dementia experience impairments in memory and learning, executive functioning, complex attention, language, perceptual-motor or visuospatial function, and social cognition."

There are several different types of dementia, with the major one being Alzheimer's disease, at about two-thirds of the cases. Then you have vascular dementia, Lewy body dementia, frontotemporal dementia as the next most common types. There are several others that make up the last small percentage. Besides the different types, people can also have a mix of more than one of these. Although the ratio varies from study to study, women are at a higher likelihood of developing the disease with the exception of vascular dementia where men are more likely to get that form.

You can find numerous "causes" of dementia, such as being considered type 3 diabetes (it is gaining much traction in the medical field); a build up of plaque, metals, or minerals that the brain didn't purge, like aluminum or fluoride; inactivity or lack of use of the brain; hypertension; and severe stress, and we haven't started to touch on head trauma, stroke, specific medications, alcohol, or any other exterior factors. Recent studies have shown there is more weight in modifiable factors such as one's lifestyle than solely whether the person has a genetic disposition to the disease.

In 2025, an estimated 7.2 million Americans were living with Alzheimer's (Alzheimer's Association). Less than half of geriatric doctors in the United States are comfortable with diagnosing any form of dementia. That would be like over half of the pediatric doctors not diagnosing croup. It may be in part due to the lack of a single affordable definitive test. In addition, the typical signs overlap with other conditions such as nutrient deficiencies, side effects of medications, dehydration, urinary tract infections, sleep disorders, and depression, to name a few. Or it could have something to do with how the insurance companies are willing to pay versus how it should be coded—but let's not dive into the fractured socialized medical situation in the USA: that won't get us anywhere. With such a terrible disease, wouldn't you want to know if you had even the beginning stages so you could take proactive measures in slowing the disease or to be treated by a professional?

One of the tricky parts of dementia is that the signs might not be dementia or there may be other signs. Some of the possible signs to notice:

- Memory loss, more common is short-term or recent memory loss
- Confusion with familiar tasks
- Poor judgment, mood changes, or impulsive behavior
- Language difficulties such as following a conversation, struggling with vocabulary, oddly long pauses in the middle of a conversation and possibly having no idea how to continue or repeating themselves

There are several other signs of dementia, but this disease, like many others, is best to diagnose early for greatest results and life quality. Unlike many other diseases, they have yet to find a confirmed cure, at least as of the publication date of this book. The sooner you are diagnosed, the more options are available. Once you get into the moderate range or worse, it turns into throwing sandbags at a flooded stream. It won't stop it, but it may slow the inevitable.

For links to more signs of dementia, see the chapter titled "Helpful Resources."

There are several things that claim to stave off dementia or help prevent it, some of which are things to be done at a younger age or prior to showing signs of the disease. Many that can be found in books or online are moderately simple changes to your routine, such as a healthier diet, exercise, and mental stimulation. Although, then you get into the question: was it the similarities of that task or the commonalities of the overall lifestyle? Who can tell for sure, but if they are simple and possibly for the betterment of your well-being, wouldn't it be worth a try?

How Do You Know If It Is Dementia?

As stated earlier, the typical symptoms overlapping with so many other issues is part of the reason why there is such a missed opportunity to catch dementia in an early stage. Some of these issues are vitamin deficiencies, depression, stress, urinary tract infections, side effects of any current medications, sleep disorders, thyroid problems, and dehydration.

So before you jump on the dementia bandwagon, rule these out. Most of these have more easily accessible tests and are typically reversible. This would be a great spot to start. In fact, I pray this is as far as you need to traverse on this journey because it's something treatable and reversible and not dementia at all.

You can start this conversation with your provider by saying something like, "I've experienced some cognitive issues recently, and I'd like to have a few tests run to see if I have..." Pick one of the items listed above or another that may be likely for you or the situation. A few of the above can possibly be ruled out just by adopting a healthier habit or two.

Allow your provider the opportunity to give more options. Ask open-ended questions. They are the professionals and have a font of knowledge that is waiting to be tapped.

Ruby's Story

I wonder when I first noticed that many of my mother's usually endearing traits might be something more, something other than who she was. She was always funny, selfless, quirky, and stubborn—a truly eccentric woman. Her most endearing trait, of course, was her kindness to friends and strangers alike. Unfortunately, scrupulous people prey on our elders, and she was scammed quite a few times—online, on her telephone, and even with people coming to her door. She lived alone in the home I grew up in. She was there a total of fifty-seven years, ten of them after my father died. Her plan was to live there until she died.

As with any other person, age took a natural toll on my mother's health. My father passed away in 2010, and about a year later, Mom began having heart problems (a genetic gift). Several times, I drove to her house to collect her, and then we'd drive to the ER, always reminding her to phone an ambulance first and then me. Over time, it was clear she would never do this, so I would phone them for her. I took her to all appointments so I could ask questions *and* because driving on the freeway made her nervous. She signed the appropriate paperwork so I could have access to her medical records, order her medications, and communicate with her doctors. ***I highly encourage doing this before things get more difficult.***

Her doctor, Dr. M, was wonderful, and she adored him as much as he seemed to care for her. At several appointments over the years, he'd give her some basic questions to answer, and she did okay, not great but okay. She'd ask if her brain was good, and his reply was always, "You're doing great. I hope I'm doing as well as you when I am your age." She was so proud of this. I guess he didn't notice that before answering basic questions about her health, she *always* looked to me for answers. I learned to look down so we wouldn't make eye contact, hoping she would be able to answer the questions herself. Or perhaps he was like the majority of general practitioners who aren't comfortable diagnosing a patient with dementia.*[1]

In May 2019, my mother was carrying a bucket of rocks from one side of her yard to another. Normal behavior for all eighty-four-year-olds, right? She tripped and fell forward, with both wrists landing underneath her, clasping the bucket

---

1. https://www.powershealth.org/about-us/newsroom/health-library/2025/01/21/most-dementia-patients-unaware-of-diagnosishttps://pmc.ncbi.nlm.nih.gov/articles/PMC12206097

handle. She banged her head on the concrete, chipped a tooth, and missed hitting her head on a large plant pot by mere inches. Lying there for a few minutes, she composed herself enough to stand, turning two doorknobs with shattered wrists, and phoned 911. She would have phoned me, as she had done for every other medical emergency, but I was out of the country visiting in-laws.

She needed three wrist surgeries over the next month and immediate 24/7 care because you can do absolutely nothing for yourself with two broken wrists. Nothing. A dear friend stayed with her for a week until I got home, then for the next six weeks, I lived with her. She seemed off—unclear, impatient, disheveled—but I put it all down to the strong pain relievers she was taking and her "I can take care of myself" personality.

During this time, Mom was very impatient. If I was too slow doing something, she would stand on one foot and try to use her other to do whatever she deemed urgent. I got very little sleep over those six weeks because she got up multiple times in the night to go to the bathroom. I mean eight or nine times. I had to assist because, well... two broken wrists.

I also caught her one night trying to refill her water glass to take some acetaminophen for her pain. I recorded each dose of pain medication I gave her and the exact time it was given. No doses were missed. The prescription medications were in a location only I knew, but after that night, I also had to hide her over-the-counter pain meds, including those in her bathroom medicine cabinets.

At some point over the years, she had transferred pills into easy-to-open unlabeled bottles instead of the child- and elder-proof bottles the pills came in. I read that many seniors overdose on OTC medications. I can see why. That night, she could not remember being given any pain medication, and again, I put it down to the strength of her narcotic medications. It was at this time I began taking over filling her pill boxes because I had noticed that, prior to her fall, the pills placed in each day were often missing a dose or contained twice the required dose. I purchased different-colored pill boxes labeled by days of the week and AM and PM. I wanted to keep it as simple as possible for her when I eventually returned home.

Funny, not at all funny story… My mother had great health insurance, and I reached out to them to see if we could have any home help during this time. Had she broken both legs, they would've sent someone to help. Because it was both wrists, she didn't qualify for any assistance. I was shocked, and I think the woman relaying the information to me was also. I tried to explain the situation more clearly: "She can't cook, feed herself, bathe herself, dress herself, wipe her own bottom even, but she doesn't qualify? She could do everything I just mentioned with two broken legs, although bathing would be difficult, but still, that is unbelievable."

"I'm sorry. Is there anything else I can help you with?"

"No. Thank you."

Our healthcare system is ridiculous. What if I didn't live nearby? What if I wasn't able to move in with her? It's easy to see how so many seniors fall through the cracks.

Mom wasn't happy that I didn't return her car keys straight away when I moved out, but her wrists needed to heal before she could grip a steering wheel properly. I wanted her to keep her independence but had to consider other drivers as well. I noticed several little dings in her car, and she always had an excuse and put the blame on other drivers. Perhaps the dings weren't her fault, but I believed they were, especially as her stories around acquiring them changed.

Because of her broken wrists, she was unable to write checks, so I started paying her bills and making all of her medical appointments as well. Made sense since I would be the one driving her to the appointments. By paying her bills, I also learned how many people and organizations she was happily writing checks to each month. Each time an envelope came through the post asking for money, she'd send some, forgetting she had already done so. She got quite miffed with me when I took over because I'd remind her that she had already donated to an organization and she was adamant she hadn't done so for months or years even. The check stubs told a different story. The first few weeks, several checks (written before her accident) came back unsigned, or with differing amounts in numbers and words. Or they had no stamp or an incomplete address.

I had no idea she was struggling with these basic things. My mother taught her

Sunday school class, volunteered at a clothes closet and her church library, went to yoga at a senior center, and was her neighborhood watch chairperson. She also did crosswords and Sudoku and read a lot. Her life was full, and she lunched with friends, used social media, and talked on her telephone for hours on end.

Somehow, we survived one another for those six weeks. I guess both of us being stubborn helped with that, but I know she was relieved when I packed my bags and went home.

As her wrists healed and with my additional help of paying her bills and keeping on top of her medications, her life seemed to be getting back on track. She was once again driving to and from her church, the places she volunteered, and the grocery store. They were all within a two-mile radius of her home and required no freeway driving.

After this first bad fall in 2019, I put a deposit on a senior community being built right next door to her church. The plans included a shuttle service that she would be able to take to church, the grocery store, and even some organized outings. Mom was a social butterfly, and the community included a library, a pool, beautiful outdoor spaces, a movie theater, a beauty salon, a cleaner who came by weekly, etc... It was pet friendly, and she'd even have her own backyard. Best of all, she could live independently in a two-bedroom ADA-compliant duplex. A button needed to be pressed every morning by a certain time to check in or someone from the office would come to check on her. If in trouble, there was a red cord in each bathroom to call for help. The gated community would be locked at night but open during the day. I thought it sounded great. Mom went back and forth about moving there, but while it was being built, I tried to make it sound positive. Her home had too many stairs, too many levels, too many places to trip. She argued that she knew her neighbors. She did, but there were people she already knew moving into this new community also. It brought some comfort to me knowing she would be in an environment made specifically for seniors.

When Covid struck, I had to convince her to stop going out. Like many seniors, she didn't really grasp the severity of the virus. She'd forget and carry on with her volunteer duties. And wearing a mask on her chin wasn't going to cut it, so I had to ask for her car keys to keep her from going anywhere. I think lockdown contributed to her deteriorating mental acuity. But we couldn't see a doctor because of the lockdown. I delivered her groceries weekly and spoke with her on the phone daily.

In May of 2020, she passed out and fell down inside her home and broke her humerus (arm). When her dog had licked her awake, she phoned me, and I phoned an ambulance. As in the past, I instructed her to put her dog in her bedroom and unlock the front door for the paramedics. I then phoned one of her wonderful neighbors and asked them to wait with her, or at least let her dog out of the bedroom and lock her house up after Mom had been taken away. I met her at the hospital.

After this fall, my husband and I thought it would be best to bring Mom and her dog into our home to look after her. True, she had only broken one arm and might only need someone to stay with her for a few days to administer medications and assist, but the doctors couldn't say what caused her to pass out. This was scary and it might happen again. Next time, it could happen outside, or she might hit her head. So once checked out from the hospital, she came to our house. This way, my husband and I could share the load, and it would really help both Mom's and my own mental health. I also thought Mom might not get so argumentative with me if my spouse was there. Besides, he's a great cook, and she always loved whatever he prepared.

I was mistaken. She was not happy to come stay with us. She wanted to go home. The choice I gave her was going to her house with me, to collect her dog and some personal items, *or* I would drive her straight to my house and then go to hers alone. I guess I hadn't realized that a shift had been taking place for some time now. I was parenting my mother, which she deeply resented. It was difficult for me also.

Our home was built in 1910 and has a Jack and Jill bathroom between two bedrooms. We shared this bathroom with Mom. As before, she got up multiple times a night to go to the bathroom. She also packed and unpacked on a daily basis with her uninjured arm. I gave her a space for her toiletries in the bathroom to make her feel comfortable, but she continued to put things away. She would fret because she didn't have her toothbrush or hairbrush with her, and I would find them packed away in a zipper of her suitcase or stuffed into a sock.

Her behavior reminded me of some things that had started a few years prior. My mom was from Arkansas and visited family and friends once a year. She usually flew to an airport where her sister would board the plane. They'd travel together the rest of the way and pick up a rental car. Beginning in 2016, at her request, I traveled with her. It made sense for me to be their driver, as they were both getting older. We'd meet her sister, fly to Arkansas, and then I would be their driver for the next ten days or so. She used to misplace things on those trips and become quite distressed and insist she didn't have whatever item was missing. Her reactions were extreme. I'd find the items in different compartments of her handbag, suitcase, or dresser drawers. At the time, I didn't put it down to much besides her quirky personality and the natural forgetfulness of age. Oh, hindsight.

I did try to talk with her sister about it a few times because she was younger and witnessing these behaviors. She would shut me down immediately, usually by saying, "Well, we all forget things sometimes. She's just fine."

This was to become a common response from relatives and friends of Mom's. Especially people close to her age. They saw the independent, fun, busy woman. It was either difficult for them to see what was happening, or they didn't want to see it. Perhaps it frightened them?

Because of her 2020 accident, Mom was absorbed into our Covid bubble, which might have been a good thing to help with her not being so lonely. Eating meals with her, we noticed a lot of choking on food. Her short-term memory and repetition of questions suggested there was a bit more going on than senior forgetfulness. Being in the midst of Covid meant I couldn't get her in to see her doctor until January of 2021.

When the orthopedic surgeon gave Mom the all clear to return to her own home, I spoke with him about her arm and hand strength and how it might affect her reflexes and driving. I did this in front of Mom, as I wanted to be as transparent as possible and not hide anything from her. He agreed she was getting too old to drive (safely), and she took his advice very well. Once back at her house, I gently asked for the second set of car keys I knew she had somewhere else in her house. That made her very angry. She retrieved them and slammed them down on the table in front of me, revealing a temper I had never seen before. I guess she thought she could drive without my knowledge? I'm not sure if all seniors get sneaky when they realize they aren't able to be as independent as they once were or if it's a part of dementia. Might be a little of both. I assured her I would continue to help with her grocery shopping, and I promised to pick her up and take her to the church she attended when lockdown ended. I also reminded her that she had friends who would be more than happy to pick her up for lunch dates when it was safe to do so.

Driving to Mom's house weekly to fill her medication containers wasn't giving me the most confidence she was safely getting what she needed and at the correct times. I'd still find skipped meds or some pills rearranged into the wrong days or even the odd pill on the floor. I learned about a carousel that I could fill with meds to be dispensed however and whenever I set it. There was an app for my phone so I could follow along and receive notifications. There were still ways she could miss a dose, but an alarm would continue to sound every fifteen minutes, and I would get an alert on my phone so I could phone and remind her. I recommend some sort of medication dispenser for any senior living alone. It definitely helps and makes it really difficult for them to take too many of their meds or skip doses. There was no way for her to access the pills until they were dispensed, so unless she hoarded them, she couldn't overdose.

In October 2020, prior to her dementia diagnosis, we moved Mom and her dog, Max, into that beautiful senior community duplex. It was gorgeous. When lockdown ended, she joined a book club immediately and began organizing the library. Of course, there were a few disagreements as to how the books should be arranged with other equally stubborn seniors, but it still occupied her time. In addition to quite a few members of her church living in the community, she made a very dear new friend, whom I'll call Jackie.

Jackie was a few years older than Mom, and her family didn't live nearby. She was happy to be taken under Mom's mother-hen wing and introduced to her church class as well as others in the community. These two women would swim and walk together. It was all great until one very hot day, over 100 degrees Fahrenheit, they thought a walk to a "nearby" shop would be a good idea. They didn't realize it was about a mile away, with no shade en route, and hadn't worn hats or taken any water with them. They arrived at their destination and bought some water. Somehow, they made it home, but I shudder to think of the potential mishaps that might have happened. Mom thought it was funny that they'd forgotten their hats and water. She told me all about the ordeal, laughing as she relayed it.

When January 2021 arrived, her beloved Dr. M was out on leave. The doctor who we met noticed immediately that Mom was struggling with her memory. Not knowing my mother, she was observing her purely from a medical point of view, not a personal one, as Dr. M had been doing. She asked pointed questions and then referred us to a neurologist for further testing. To this day, I am thankful there was an interim physician. The neurologist tested Mom, asked us both a lot of questions, and then told us that, based on the test results, Mom had Alzheimer's. She said it was in the early to middle stages. Because of other meds Mom took, she couldn't take any of the medications that might help slow down the disease. We were given a packet about the stages of Alzheimer's. It also included simple chair or wall exercises to do and suggested foods to eat often: blueberries and leafy greens. That was it.

I phoned six months later because the behaviors were changing quite a lot. They asked if I thought Mom was in danger of hurting herself or anyone else. When I said no, they said they'd see me in January of 2022. A year from the first diagnosis. No one contacted us to make that appointment, so I made it. As with the primary care physician, there was an interim neurologist. This doctor had pulled all brain scans from Mom's past and showed us where on her brain the dementia had begun, ten years prior to her diagnosis, and how it had grown. Would things have been different had we known earlier? Perhaps Mom could've started on medication that may have slowed down her disease. We will never know, but it does make me wonder why it seems so very difficult for a dementia diagnosis, especially of an elderly person.

This neurologist also prescribed an extremely low-dose antidepressant because Mom had gotten very tearful and erratic with her moods. He said it should help her sleep better as well. It helped with her depression a bit but not her sleeping pattern. As time went on, we had to increase the dosage for the antidepressant and introduce sleeping medication.

Because Mom didn't understand she could no longer safely do everything in life she had once done, she revealed things she might have otherwise withheld from me, although she still tried to hide some things. Usually, I figured them out or she'd accidentally let them slip. I caught her in several mistruths. She'd be embarrassed and if I asked any questions, she'd say, "I don't know. I don't know." She cried a lot. I think it must have scared her.

I tried to understand this and would often say, "I'm sorry this is happening, Mom. It must be frightening for you."

Her response was "It's fine." She did not want to talk about it.

I came to learn that she *had* told some of her friends about her dementia but not others. Was she embarrassed, did she really not understand, or did she just forget? I'm not sure. She'd talk about friends and family members who had been diagnosed with Alzheimer's or Parkinson's disease with concern and understanding. But she'd always say, "I think (insert name) is having memory problems. I'm worried about them." The way she talked about them made me think she didn't think of herself as being the same.

I guess I'm telling you all of this so you might recognize the signs. If left up to the health professionals, it can be really tricky. Without a health advocate, which I was for my mom, I've no idea how much worse things would've become before we had any idea of how to assist her.

Once Mom was diagnosed with Alzheimer's, we knew it was only a matter of time before she couldn't live independently. While she lived in the senior community, we began work on our detached garage, turning it into a 675 ft ADU (accessory dwelling unit), or granny flat. We built it using money from the sale of Mom's house. She said she'd rather do that than live in a care home.

It was across our backyard and would still provide Mom with the independence she desperately wanted to keep while we looked after her.

My husband and I mainly worked from home so were able to offer round-the-clock care, whilst allowing a bit of space between all of us. Mom still felt she had some independence, and we were close enough and popping in frequently to make sure everything was okay. I realize that not everyone is in a position to build or even make a place for their loved one to live in. Even if they come to live in your home, there are a lot of safety issues that need to be taken into consideration. We learned all of these as we went along. You can find a list in the chapter titled "Caregivers."

Our lives settled into a routine. I would go down every morning, prepare breakfast, and help Mom choose some weather-appropriate clothing. Through research, we learned a lot of dementia patients wear unsuitable clothes for the weather. Many even remove their clothing altogether. We had also dispersed with the medicine carousel, as Mom now found it confusing. We were able to give her the meds twice a day, and make sure she took them and didn't misplace or throw them out. For safety, we still kept the medications in our home.

Once settled, Mom could have her morning to herself—drink her cocoa, read her newspaper or a book, do a crossword, watch the news—all within her own time frame, the same way she had since retiring twenty-plus years ago. Many people with dementia crave sweets, and my mother was no exception. I had to limit sweets and, for my mother, hot cocoa, or she'd go through all of it in a few hours. I'd make her one drink in the morning and then leave only one packet for her to make later.

My husband would go down to her cottage and make her lunch a few hours later. Sometimes one of us would eat with her, but she liked to eat quite early, so one or both of us would just sit and visit while she ate. This also meant we could make sure the dog didn't get her meals.

Dinner was a family affair (again, too early to eat for us). Hubby would cook while I assisted Mom in the shower, using a stool for safety. These were the times she was the most vulnerable. She would cry as I bathed her, repeating over and over again, "I'm so sorry. I don't want to be a burden." I'd remind her she was not a burden and that she had taken care of me when I was young and now I was taking care of her.

We realized that following a routine was best, so breakfast was at 7 am, lunch at 11:30, dinner at 5:30, and she'd usually go to bed at 7 pm. If we turned up even five minutes late, she would make an attempt to prepare her own meal, but sadly, she was no longer able to do so. When we'd arrive to find this, she'd tell us it was because she hadn't eaten all day or for a few days, etc... This continued until she died. She could not remember eating.

There were walks around the neighborhood together, visits to the free libraries dotted about, church to attend, and lunch with friends. Either they'd bring it by or the brave ones took her out. I had to explain to them that she could not be left alone *ever* because she would forget where she was and wander off. The gates to our backyard were both locked. Mom asked for the keys multiple times, saying she wanted to go here or there. Sometimes she got mad even though I tried to gently explain that we kept them locked for her safety. She even asked my brother to make her a set of keys but not tell me.

She loved to talk on the phone with her sisters and friends, but I noticed these calls lessened, as did the visits from most of her friends. I think many people don't know how to be around someone with dementia. A few told me it was just too difficult to repeat the same thing or hear the same thing over and over again. I knew it was exhausting. It may have also highlighted painful memories or fears of what might be to come. Even my brother was unable to grasp it. He spoke to Mom on the phone most days, and he'd phone me up afterward very upset, telling me what she had said and saying he just wanted her to get better. I'd explain that she said those things because of her dementia and that she was not going to get better, only worse as the disease progressed.

To keep Mom safe, and for our own peace of mind, we put a camera in her living room. It covered that room, her kitchen, and the front and side doors of her cottage. It did not cover the bedroom or bathroom. I showered Mom, so I wasn't too worried about her falling in the shower. I wanted to give her as much privacy as possible also. Mom's paranoia was growing, and she would close all blinds facing our home, sometimes even pinning sheets on top of them for extra darkness. I asked if the light hurt her eyes, but she said it didn't. From the beginning, even before she became paranoid, I decided not to tell her about the camera. As it sat high on a shelf, I told her it was a carbon monoxide monitor. I don't feel bad about telling her that. Had Mom not had dementia, there would be no need for a camera. It meant I could check on her, look back at her behavior throughout the night, and get to her quickly if she fell, which she did more than once. At night, she got up a dozen times, sometimes five minutes apart, going into the bathroom, getting a drink of water from the kitchen, and sometimes just staring out the open door or a window, or at a wall. Because she was not sleeping well at night, she usually slept many daytime hours in her recliner. Although, she vehemently denied any naps. "I was just watching the news or reading" was a common refrain when we'd walk in to prepare a meal and find her sleeping comfortably with her dog on her lap.

I made a vow to myself that once Mom was no longer able to walk, I would find other care for her. She had an old back injury coupled with osteoporosis, which meant a broken vertebrae in her spine. The first time back problems resurfaced, a few weeks in rehab and another five weeks in a board and care facility were enough to have her back home, using a walker, with a wheelchair for any longer outings. She had regular visits from PT (physical therapy) and OT (occupational therapy) during this time, but on days they weren't there, I'd do the exercises with her or she wouldn't do them. I think she'd given up as opposed to forgetting them because each time I tried to do them with her, she complained and always hid the exercise sheet.

The therapists stopped coming because they said she was non-compliant. She was. Trying to keep a back brace on an already stubborn person with dementia is something I'd wish upon no one. Ever. During this time, the camera came in really handy. I'd see no brace or a loose brace and make my way to the cottage with some made-up excuse, only to "discover" her brace needed to be refitted. It was such a challenging six months, and I was grateful when she no longer needed the brace. It did give me an insight into what was to come.

I'm sure it varies by state, but in our state, I had less than a day to choose a rehab center to go to from the hospital and forty-eight hours to find a board and care facility when her insurance ran out for rehab. A hospital social worker put us in touch with someone who we used as a go-between. We were fortunate to find a wonderful place the first time. Not so fortunate a year later when Mom had a stroke. I truly wish someone had given me a list. I learned by trial and error. I'll add some questions to ask and things to look out for at the end. These can be found in the chapter titled "When Looking for a Care Home."

There were other falls with a bleeding head and trips to the ER. Waiting to be seen with a dementia patient is awful. Mom didn't understand why we were there, kept telling us she was ready to go home, and then told the doctors all kinds of reasons as to what happened. She also told every single medical person she ever met that she had been a runner. They'd engage and ask when. Her pat reply was, "I stopped running a few miles a day about a month ago."

In the ER, I asked if her dementia was listed on her medical record. It wasn't. I think a lot of confusion could have been avoided if dementia patients were given a special colored hospital bracelet or had a small purple color on their record. Every person approaching them and asking questions would understand, as opposed to getting conflicting answers and then having to clarify with me. Several nurses agreed that this would make their jobs easier. Other serious medical conditions show up on ER charts; why doesn't dementia?

People with dementia have a lot of different behaviors, but there *are* many that are similar. That being said, what works for one person's behavior might work only temporarily for another person's, or never work at all. Each case is different, as is each day. You think you've found a routine and then you need to adjust again as their dementia progresses.

If something you try doesn't work, remember it isn't anything you've done wrong. Give yourself some grace.

I mentioned a stroke earlier. I was showering Mom when this happened. An ambulance was with us within fifteen minutes. After a few nights in the hospital, Mom was to be put into another rehabilitation facility. Again, I had to choose one quickly. There are no tours for this. A hospital social worker gives you the facilities with openings and you go online, read reviews, say a prayer, and choose one. It is only temporary, but you still want the best you can get. I found that the two I chose were tired looking, no longer fancy as you imagined they once were, but both of these facilities had very caring staff. There, she would work with a wheelchair and walker.

Tip: Label every single item of clothing and collect and do their laundry yourself if you ever want to see their items again. Or only send items you are okay with losing. These places are busy and dealing with hundreds of people with mild to severe needs. A social worker advised me to do my own laundry. I put a hamper in her closet with a large sign on the door that her family was doing her laundry. It was good advice and mostly worked. I was visiting daily so I could collect it every two or three days.

I'd try to visit during meal times to help Mom eat. She was receiving PT, OT, and speech therapy. The latter often took place during one of her meals. With Mom focused on holding her utensils, she didn't feel the pressure when speaking with the speech therapist that she might have if focusing solely on that. She was more reliant on her wheelchair now, and PT people were working with her on using it.

After Mom's stroke, her stories that blended reality and fantasy became more vivid. We would just go along with whatever she was telling us and engage by asking questions. We never wanted her to feel embarrassed.

It is not easy to be a caregiver, and each person must be honest with themselves when considering whether or not they will try to step into this role. It's like having a toddler, but a toddler eventually learns what we are teaching them. A person with dementia isn't able to. Being full-time caregivers for my mother meant my husband and I could never have nights or vacations away. Our days and nights were on Mom's schedule. In addition to the physical and mental exhaustion of care, putting your life and relationships second to your loved one's needs is something to consider. It's a lot to ask of a relationship, and I know I'm so lucky that my husband was my partner in this.

If you have siblings, I hope they are willing to step in and share in the care. From what I've gleaned, care of an elderly parent is often done by only one child. Many people have siblings who aren't interested in the day-to-day care, or they live too far away to help. Paying for care is very expensive, and your only choice might be to keep them in your home. If this is the case, try to find someone who can occasionally help you, if only for a few hours while you run to the store or go to a movie or a class, doing something for yourself. You can prepare the meal and ask the friend to be there to give it to them or sit with them and visit. If you have these friends, they are gems and you are blessed.

After caring for Mom full time for two years, we made the decision to find her a permanent home with round-the-clock care. Be prepared for pushback from family members on this, especially if they've had nothing to do with the care and have no idea what it entails and how much it has impacted your life. They, along with everyone else, always said, "Your mom looks great. You're doing such a wonderful job taking care of her." It's a tough thing to hear. The comments were well meaning, but they just kind of rubbed me the wrong way, as in, you're doing so well, why would you ever change things?

Please, do not feel guilty when you make this decision.

If you make it early on and never become a caregiver, or if after some time has passed, you choose full-time care, do not feel guilty. You are putting the needs and safety of your loved one first. I mean this. Even if you think you are putting your own needs first because you think you will be unable to care for them, you are being honest, and that is *still* putting their needs first. This is another reason for the importance of having your family member appoint you as their power of attorney, along with their medical appointee, before they become mentally unable to make these decisions.

Okay, choosing a care home and what to look for. After experiencing the number of residents in the rehab centers, I thought Mom would benefit from living in a board and care home. California (where we are) has licensed homes that allow up to six residents. They are regular homes that have had some renovations to make them ADA accessible. They consist of full-time staff, many who live in. As before, I was given the names and addresses of homes with openings and went to tour them.

I think I could walk into a board and care home now and easily spot the fraudsters out to make money over the genuinely caring folks. This, sadly, wasn't always the case, and there were several trial and errors, from which I was able to compile a short list that could help others going through the same thing. These questions and items to look for can be found in the chapter titled "When Looking for a Care Home."

This may sound daunting, but don't give up. My spouse and I had to move Mom into four homes over a two-month period until we found the right fit. Once we found it, we felt tremendous relief and knew my mother was receiving kind, loving care in a safe and healthy environment.

If you are keeping your loved one in your home, at some point you will need to find professional caregivers to come in at times. Many of these services have a minimum of two- to four-hour visits, or a certain number of hours in a week. Again, ask them as many questions as you need to. These questions can begin as you research different agencies. If you are a human or pet parent, imagine you are interviewing child or pet carers. Your loved one deserves the same amount of background research into someone who will be caring for them. Ask around. Friends might be able to recommend an agency or specific people. Read independent reviews.

These are my experiences with my mother. As previously stated, everyone's journey will be different. I hope I've shared useful information, or given you some hope—even if it's just knowing that, if you are struggling, it's normal. **Do not**

be afraid to ask for help. On Mom's third annual visit with her neurologist, I calmly stated that I felt as if we'd been left floundering and trying to figure everything out on our own. The doctor was surprised. She then apologized and said they would try to do better going forward. She was true to her word, and I had a phone call that very afternoon to set up a palliative care team, consisting of a doctor and a social worker. During a forty-five-minute telephone conversation, they listened to all of my concerns and offered some resources available to us. This was great, but I stress that I had to ask for help.

During one of Mom's hospitalizations (due to neglect from a care home), Mom's palliative care team told me it might be a good idea to ask the doctor to request hospice care. When people hear hospice, they often think it means the recipient of such care is dying soon. Sometimes they are, but hospice doesn't necessarily mean this. I asked the doctor at the hospital if he would refer Mom to hospice, and he nearly bit my head off. His exact words were, "Hospice is for someone who will die within six months. Your mother is not there yet." I was shocked and deferred to his medical opinion. I later learned that hospice will reevaluate a patient after six months and decide whether they still require the services they provide. If not, the patient will be removed from hospice. That's it. Receiving the incredible extra care that hospice can provide does NOT mean your loved one is dying. Sometimes they improve from all the extra care.

After my first hand slap, I hadn't thought about hospice again. It was a physical therapist who visited Mom regularly who phoned me up after a visit. She said, "I feel like my visits with your mother are no longer helping her. They feel more like torture. I think we should discontinue the PT. Have you considered hospice?" I told her what the doctor had said, and she professionally (without throwing the doctor under the bus) said, "Well, I think your mother would benefit from a hospice evaluation at this time." She then offered to help organize that if I wanted to proceed. I did, and what a difference it made. A doctor came, evaluated my mother to determine whether she qualified for hospice care. She did.

If you also thought hospice was only for the end, don't feel bad. Even doctors are confused. I cannot state enough how caring my mother's hospice team she had for the last three months of her life was. Being able to communicate with trained nurses and doctors who are checking on, monitoring, and administering care, on top of the already incredible care my mother received at her last care home was an extra comfort for Mom and also for us.

Ironically, when that doctor snapped at me, it was January—my mother died five months later in June. Hopefully, as his career continues, he will learn more. I can't really blame him, though, because as the elder population in the USA increases, doctors who specialize in their treatment have decreased.*[2]

If you are not satisfied with the doctor treating your loved one, ask for someone else. I think this sums up everything I've been trying to say. Ask questions. Ask for support. Ask what is available to you. Ask for a specialist.

2. https://conversationstoremember.org/geriatricians-who-they-are-why-they-are-important-and-why-we-need-morehttps://www.forbes.com/sites/howardgleckman/2026/01/26/as-numbers-of-older-adults-grow-the-supply-of-doctors-isnt-keeping-up/

June's Story

I was talking to friends whose parents went through this too. My mother was always eccentric, and some of the stories she told my grandpa, from when I was a kid, were pretty out there. Even as I got older, I couldn't find any substantiating evidence to back up those stories, and so, I wonder if she had early-onset dementia, like my friend's mom did. She used to knit and crochet, but when she got older, she couldn't do it because of her arthritis. She used to enjoy watching musicals, musical comedies, and stuff like that. Then there was a point when she didn't like the stuff she previously enjoyed, and the more her mental state degraded, the more she enjoyed watching football and golf. I now have an ongoing inside joke with my wife when someone asks me if I want to watch the Super Bowl, because of it.

They say that traumatic instances will start the process of dementia. Part of that, I think, started when I was a kid and my mom's mom moved in with us. My parents kept getting calls from the police department and hospital about my grandmother. The sheriff's office would go out to my grandmother's house, because she'd regularly call to report people watching her. I think she called about a burglar who wasn't there, which is why they did a seventy-two-hour watch on her, but I'm not sure. When they tested my granny, they were able to diagnose her with Alzheimer's because of the aluminum deposits in her brain. Apparently that's a sign of Alzheimer's: deposits of aluminium on the brain.

My family drove over nine hours, packed my granny's house up, and moved her into our home. My grandmother was with us for five or six years, and it just got worse and worse. My grandmother went backward, thinking my brother was my grandfather. They shared the same name and had a very similar face, so it wasn't a complete stretch.

During the time when my mother was taking care of my grandmother, my father was making some very bad life decisions for our whole family. Bad choices such as blowing the business up his nose, cheating on my mother with multiple women, and wasting the money from the sale of my grandmother's house on drugs and his girlfriends. So my mom was stuck dealing with my father's poor life choices, taking care of her mom with dementia, and taking care of us kids, which made her a wreck, and I think that was the beginning for her. She had a mental breakdown and didn't come back one hundred percent from that. Then granny died, and my mother never fully recovered.

I joined the Navy. Several years in, I had to come home, which was about an eight-hour drive, on emergency leave because my mother'd become septic from her kidney stones and went into a coma. They didn't think she was going to make it, but she woke up after a week. They say that traumatic instances will start dementia, then a physical problem will happen, and that'll push the disease over the edge. I think this instance was the one that caused the big fallout. After this happened, my brother helped out somewhat, as I wasn't able to be around too much.

Looking back, the other noticeable signs were how she would forget the day-to-day things. She was a great cook, but then her cooking went to crap. Like she made some scrambled eggs, and it was more like snot. She'd leave food out on the counter, and it would spoil. She would leave a can open on the table or replace the open can back into the cabinet. She would leave something on the burner and walk away. There were scorch marks on the wall behind the burner from her leaving things on. Or how she would hyper-focus on small random things. She always had cats, and there was a point when she stopped cleaning up after them, so her whole apartment smelled like tomcats. She started sleeping in her recliner because she didn't want to be in a smaller room. Along with the new claustrophobia, she'd get vertigo. But she didn't have these issues before. They had her on pills for vertigo and a lot of other different medications. Vertigo was one of the early symptoms that was really bad. She thought it was her blood pressure, but her blood pressure was never that bad or anything to constitute an issue.

I received many calls from the hospital about her falling and ending up in there. She was very good at hiding that she had anything wrong. My mother went to the hospital seven or eight times with different stuff, and they would tell us, "Your mom's a little off," but they didn't diagnose her or suggest a way to get her help. She was capable of taking care of herself, but she needed someone to check on her. Because she lived alone, the state (California) provided an aide who was supposed to come in, check on her, and help her out with the simple day-to-day stuff. And they were horrible. The only thing they did was rob her blind. They were not good people.

She got sick again and needed a blood transfusion, but she couldn't get one due to her beliefs: she was a Jehovah's Witness. My brother got upset about the situation. It was her choice; what was I supposed to do, go against her beliefs and her choice? He didn't like the fact that I was willing to let my mother die over her religion, and he claimed I was taking his kids' grandmother away from them. After she didn't get a blood transfusion, my brother stopped helping and visiting her pretty much altogether. She was showing big signs of dementia when she got home, but we were told we wouldn't be able to get a diagnosis until there was something completely red-flagged for them to get her in.

When we knew for sure, it was the similarities of what happened with my granny. My mother started seeing things. She thought someone was always watching her and looking in her window. She'd called emergency several times about how there was someone in her apartment or someone was looking in her window. A constant visual she would "see" was this woman with a yellow hat, and that was the final straw. My friend from high school was the deputy in town; he called my brother. My brother said he didn't care, and so then the deputy called my personal number. He told me she saw the lady with the yellow hat. "I'm standing right here, and she swears that somebody's here in the room with us right now. Pointing over in a spot where there's no one." Like she was having a full on psychosis. He was the one who suggested a seventy-two-hour evaluation on her to see if they could get a diagnosis, and that's how we were able to get her in, because of his recommendation.

The hospital in her town wouldn't do it. So I had to make an emergency eight-hour trip to pick her up and drive her to a different town for her to get the seventy-two hour psych evaluation. During the forty-minute drive there, the whole time she talked to me about "her good son" (me). During the evaluation, she was hiding it so well, they were planning to release her up until the last part of the third day when she started telling the doctor about how she remembered the doctor and his wife as children, and that's when they finally diagnosed it. We never got a definition on what kind of dementia she had, just that she had dementia. She'd become like a toddler, where she was capable of doing most things, but you needed someone in there to follow behind and turn things off, pick things up, or put stuff away. Then she went pretty fast, and it's like having a kid: there's no how-to manual on how to deal with a parent aging. I think it's progressive, and I think there are triggers along the way. And codependency would also be part of it; she was codependent.

The biggest surprise after she was diagnosed was how little support we got from the medical community. To be fair, she was on California Medicaid, so they kind of just said, "Ah, too bad." Not to mention the whole medical situation is so overwhelmed. The extra layers of frustration were with family and all the loose ends. My mother had been living in an apartment by herself. We had to clean it up and take care of all that when we moved her to a home. I'd found out she hadn't been paying her bills, so in order to get utilities, she had put them in my name because she had my military paperwork there. My brother, who was about a half an hour's drive away from where my mother lived, wouldn't help or lift a finger for our mom. The eight-hour drive back and forth didn't help, but I was able to move closer so the drive turned into only two hours after that.

What happened to my mother when she was taking care of my grandmother with this disease steeled my decision to not bring my mother to the house for my wife to go through that with my mom. Not only did I work ungodly hours, so my wife would have been the main caregiver; but it's not her mom, and it's not fair to her. It's not fair to anyone. We placed her in a professional care home close to my brother, per his request. The home had nursing aides but didn't have full-time residents. I wanted to move her to a place closer to me, but my brother was insistent on keeping her close to his family and in California, even though he didn't regularly visit her. In that home, they seemed to focus on keeping her drugged and docile. Although one good benefit to keeping her close to where she lived was the people in her religion would regularly visit her. They would come and take her to meeting and back, so she would get some regular visitors multiple times a week. They would even just stop by to converse with her. I don't think the religion helped, but the people of that community did.

When that home closed down, we moved her to another assisted living home. She then was inside a hospital, and there were about ten to twelve total, but it worked out because she was starting to have more health issues. The doctors were more proactive in the new home. This home did a lot of activities with them such as bingo and field trips, and it seemed to help her out quite a bit. The last two years, they had to keep her in a wheelchair because she prolapsed, and she had to constantly wear a brace, or she'd collapse into herself and look like she didn't have any bones.

Toward the end, she was getting violent, so they sent her to the city (Reno) to get a behavioral medicine change. When we visited her, she kept petting a cat in her lap that wasn't there and rocking back and forth. One thing I noticed over and over again is that music would bring back some recollection and peace to her. I played some of her favorite music: Fleetwood Mac, Pavarotti, Julio Iglesias, this and that. While in Reno, I was playing Julio Iglesias. She popped up, looked straight at me, and said "I saw him in concert, you know." It was always so weird, to see one minute she was there and then gone the next.

She passed during Covid. The night she died, she actually had a moment of lucidity. She knew who I was, but that's really common with dementia. The same thing happened with my grandmother the night before she died.

Margret's Story

Looking back, the spot when I should have noticed she was starting to show signs of dementia the most is when I went with my mother to the doctor. She was looking for a surgeon for her lumpectomy five years prior to her dementia diagnosis. She was sixty-eight at the time. We were both in the patient room when the surgeon discussed what he was planning on doing. After some questions were asked, and when we got home, I was shocked by the stories she made up about what he had planned on doing. I, personally, didn't care much for the man, and to be completely honest, he reminded me of an Eddie Izzard skit about the chiropractor, who no matter what was wrong with the person, he was going to "crack ya bones." It was pretty much the same. But that wasn't what she was relaying to everyone. She had an elaborate story of what other people had told her about their surgery, and she told everyone an embellished story about what was going to happen to her closer to what other people had said to her, not what the doctor had described. Unfortunately, embellishing stories has always been normal for as long as I've known her, so her making it out to be this crazy ordeal wasn't out of her norm, so it wasn't an obvious issue.

Or another fair sign should have been a year and a half later, when she wasn't reading her books as often or at all. I would purchase her books to read every month for the last decade and, on occasion, more than one a month. About a year and a half after her cancer surgery, she wasn't getting through books as quickly and hadn't finished one in several months. She had originally claimed she was just too busy at work, but when she had been retired for over six months and still hadn't finished any of the fourteen books I'd picked up for her, it should have been a sign. She retired from her job a few weeks after my father broke his hip, claiming she needed to take care of him. Both he and I wonder if she was using him as an excuse to retire because her job was becoming too difficult for her. With her retired, I reminded her she had a backlog of books she would now have the time to read and picked up a few more for her. They didn't get read.

More frequently, my father complained about how she wasn't remembering things and "she was getting more dingy/ditzy." It was a normal complaint from him, but he seemed to make this statement more frequently. I also found out he took over paying the bills around this time as bills were getting misplaced and not paid on-time.

When she was seventy-one, I changed jobs, and my family started to see my parents more often. That's when I noticed she seemed to have trouble recalling certain accounts. She would still embellish or outright make up situations, but some of them seemed more far fetched than what she'd typically claim before. She would pick something up, seem lost with it, and take the item to her room. The item would be an object that shouldn't normally be staged in her bedroom. I brought the subject to her attention a few times, and my concerns were cast aside.

I had her pick up my daughter from school, as I was working. When I got home, my oldest begged me to never have her grandmother pick her up again. She had been afraid of what might happen in the car with her grandmother due to several problems with her driving. My mother's driving was erratic, and she was freaking out about trying to turn off her blinker that she couldn't turn off without assistance from my daughter. My daughter said she'd rather wait several hours after school and have me pick her up after I was done with work than to ride with her grandmother again. I thought my daughter was being overdramatic, but when I saw some of the same examples driving with my mother, I knew my daughter's descriptions were valid.

I realized after a few months of seeing my parents more often that her current primary care physician (Dr. N.) wasn't taking care of her normal health issues, and took this as an opportunity to find a doctor who specialized in geriatric patients so they could hopefully do tests to see what was the reason she was having memory issues. Since I had questions, I went with her to the new geriatric doctor (Dr. T.). I found part of the reason why Dr. N. likely didn't catch her other medical issues, because she kept giving excuses for them. Her ears were plugged, she had a sinus infection, the stenosis in her throat had gotten worse, and her vision was cloudy. I was hoping with more oxygen to the body as well as the brain, the ability to hear, the ability to fully see again, and the lack of being sick would stop her from seeming so foggy. She would get dizzy spells to the point they gave her medication for the vertigo. (I thought it might be an inner ear thing or a lack of nutrients or even water, and we told Dr. T. about that too.) I also started going with her to the grocery store and helped her pick out better food options.

A friend of mine had recently gone through similar issues with her mother regarding dementia, and she informed me there was a test they typically have them take starting at age 65. So after remedying the other medical issues of my mother's didn't solve the problem, I brought up my concerns to Dr. T. and asked if she would have her take the dementia test. If she was starting to get a form of dementia, like her mother had, hopefully she could get early treatment or find out what was going on. The doctor, at first, was surprised that at seventy-two my mother hadn't taken the test yet and gave her the test. The problem was they had a nurse who hadn't administered the test before and had her administer it without giving her any guidance. A thirty-question test, and the nurse blatantly gave my mother over ten percent of the answers. To top it off, the nurse then helped out considerably with another quarter of the test.

It isn't entirely the nurse's or the practice's fault; she had some decent evasive excuses for why she didn't know things. For example, that day in the lobby she had to ask for the date twice and once in the patient's room with the nurse. Then when taking the test, her excuse for not knowing the date was: "Oh well, since I've been retired, I haven't had to pay attention to the date, and I never know what day it is." The question which hospital we were in: "They keep changing the name of the hospital. Who can keep up?" Or a response for what surgeries she had had in the past and for what: "There have been so many and they were so long ago, it's so hard to keep track."

So the test was botched, and nothing came of it. I asked if there was more that could be done, such as exercise and certain foods, anything. The doctor agreed that exercise would be good to do and proper eating. I saw the signs, and I didn't see why the doctor didn't. I almost contemplated that it may be a normal part of aging, even though I knew better.

I expressed my frustration to an aunt, who suggested a few supplements from a doctor who specialized in dementia, and we started having her take those. However, I found out several months later she wasn't taking them and her prescribed medication as consistently as she'd claimed.

My mother had missed her oncologist's appointment, three times in eight months, so I went with her to the engagement. During that meeting, I found out two of the common side effects of the medication she was taking to help prevent the recurrence of cancer were memory loss and osteoporosis, both of which were occurring for my mother. However, the doctor was unaware of the memory issue due to my mother not saying anything. Even though she had missed three consecutive appointments prior to the one we went to. He was only aware of the osteoporosis, as there was an easy test for it done yearly. Even with the side effects, the doctor suggested she take it for an additional two years to drop the fifteen percent of reoccurrence down to a seven percent chance of reoccurrence.

A cousin informed me about an online class that people living with dementia could take. It ran for several weeks and had worksheets and activities for them to do to help them out. The caveat was my mother needed to be able to take the class and do the tasks on her own. She signed up for it and unfortunately only went to a handful of the classes. She was having difficulty getting into the Zoom room, checking the email, turning on the computer, which prevented her from getting into the online class. We had gone through this several times, and I tried to make it as easy as possible, especially since I wouldn't be there every time the class was held. Looking back, she likely was far too gone at the time to do most of it. She looked at the activity book, didn't do any but would look at it.*[1] The link for the activity book can be found in the chapter titled "Helpful Resources that are Spots to Start" section of this book.

---

1. https://deerprogram.org/dementia-self-management/

I brought up the loss of memory every time I took her to Dr. T. for the next year and a half with no change. Each time, I kept trying to find a different way to explain my concerns, hoping to get my point across, thinking that maybe I was being obtuse and I needed to say it a different way for her to understand my concerns. It was only after my mother's insurance deemed the hospital the geriatric doctor worked at was no longer a covered provider that we changed providers.

The first visit with the new doctor (Dr. P.) I, once again, expressed my worries about her memory. Each time she would deny and fight me about it. They also administered the test, and during the visit, Dr. P. commented that he could see memory seemed to be an issue with the information she hadn't filled out or couldn't remember. And how I seemed a bit upset about the memory situation. She couldn't remember the medications she took and no longer had the several paper lists of them in her purse, two of which I added into her purse and another in her wallet a month prior. We set up another appointment to go back to the new doctor in two weeks, when we would bring her medication list so he could do a better new-patient assessment.

A few days after the first new doctor's visit, she had a heart attack at home. It is an unsettling feeling to walk into a room with your rock of a father yelling in an unsteady voice. You come to help and see him hunched over your mother lying on the tile floor. Her eyes wide open and dry as she's unresponsive on the ground. I assessed the situation, called 911, and started CPR—thanks to my years of being certified in first aid and CPR. The paramedics were able to get there pretty quickly and administered two shocks to get her out of V-fib. They ended up medevacking her to the city, where they were able to stabilize her.

The week she was in the hospital recovering, my father decided to declutter her room and office. He found several of her pills scattered about, in addition to other over-the-counter pills mixed together and not labeled, amongst other items not needing to be in her room. It was discussed for us to take over the dispensing of medications when she returned home. We had argued with my mother prior to this incident, and the best we could do was ask her if she'd taken her medication, not to mention she had extra medication in her cupboard that she wasn't taking but still had in the same location as the rest. The hospital my mother was staying in was over an hour's drive away, and I was still trying to take care of my school-age children, working, , and going up to see her with my father every day.

The first day she was intubated, and because of her stenosis, they didn't want to take it out too soon, as it was difficult to get the tube down her throat in the first place. The days following, while she was at the hospital, she was very confused. She kept pulling her cords out. She was seeing children and "bad" people. My mother didn't know or understand why she was there and why she couldn't go home. The seeing people faded after five days, but her confusion was still present. On the sixth day, they said she could go home since she would be more comfortable there and, hopefully, less confused.

I had changed to a part-time job, as juggling taking care of my children and my parents would have been quite taxing with a full-time, out-of-the-house paying job. A friend suggested that, since I was doing the majority of care, I should look into seeing if I could get paid for some of the work. When I had a little more time, I checked into it. Unfortunately, my parents made too much in social security for me to qualify to be compensated for my time. I guess they just expected me to drain my retirement or mooch off my parents.

After my mother arrived home, a speech therapist came to the house who suggested a few activities and websites. One activity was to remember three words a day. Throughout the day, ask about the three words that were decided on at the beginning of the day. If they can't remember, don't give the words outright but give them hints to recall the words. When that gets too difficult, keep the same three all week. Additionally, the hospital sent home care paperwork with a list of medications and when to give each to her. This was so helpful, and they update and print it out every time we go to an appointment—this is so great!

Once we returned to see Dr. P., he had her take the dementia test again and diagnosed her with moderate dementia. There was so much relief and vindication, it was hard not to cry that someone finally was listening to the worries and we could move to the next stage: treatment. He also offered for her to see a neurologist who specialized in patients with dementia. He started her on medication to help stall the process, as once you get into the moderate stage, there currently isn't much you can do but try to retard it. After the relief ebbed, frustration peaked its head, recalling all of the times over the last few years. I thought back, wondering if I could have gotten her in sooner or if the doctor a year and a half ago had taken my worries more seriously, could she have had a better quality of life with a better cognitive output than she does now? Likely so, but unfortunately it's too late for what ifs.

I sent a message to a friend of mine whose mother went through the same thing. He sent me a picture, saying it helped him when he was going through the thick of it with his mother. I tried to look up the website, but it was gone. This is what the text said:

LIVING WITH DEMENTIA

1. Agree, never argue

2. Divert, never reason

3. Distract, never shame

4. Reassure, never lecture

5. Reminisce, never say "remember"

6. Repeat, never say "I told you"

7. Do what they can do, never say "you can't"

8. Ask, never demand

9. Encourage, never condescend

10. Reinforce, never force

With Dr. P. and the neurologist, progress moved quickly. She was given medication to slow the decay, they gave suggestions for her to work on, and they scheduled an MRI for her brain. Both her primary and the neurologist were working with her and offered extensive support and places to go to find exercises, mental and physical, for her to do. The neurologist also gave me a go-ahead to contact her when I needed more help or when I wanted to put her into a care facility. I knew it was a sliding scale, but the loss of my mother slowed down considerably. She wouldn't get back to where she was, but she had more extended moments of lucidity than before she was on the medication. I believe, since she was no longer in denial, she worked with the family more.

My mother was quite sarcastic, but with this disease, it was hard to tell if she was actually serious or her personality was peeking out through the veil.

One of the most frustrating parts of dealing with this situation is the lack of understanding everyone else has about it. The lack of tact that people have, and I'm sure they're trying to be nice, but it comes off as callous and insulting. Unfortunately the whole concept of dementia is misunderstood for so many. "She's doing so well," "Your mother's looking good," and another one of my favorites, "You know she'll remember what you're doing for her." The fact that people try to help out when they know nothing, for me, hurts more than if they didn't say anything or just said, "That's a bummer." People need to understand the concept. They are compared to children, but you can teach children. This, however, is the slow deletion of a hard drive.

For example: when I was venting to a friend on how my mother was having problems even answering her cell phone. My friend misunderstood the concept and suggested I call my mother’s cell phone over and over again to drill the muscle memory so my mother can relearn how to answer the phone. For my friend to better understand what was going on, I demonstrated an example of one of the memory activities I play with my mother more than once a day. It is to recall the three words that we've set up for the week and it goes something like this:

"Okay, Mom, what are your three words for the week?”

"Oh, you're going to have me do that again? Uh, I don't know."

"Yes, Mom, we do them every morning. The theme for this week was frozen treats, so what are your three words?"

"Ice cream."

I'd wait for more of a response, but once it was obvious she wouldn't continue, I'd respond, "Yes, ice cream is one. What are the other two?"

"Rudolf."

"That was one a few weeks back. We want the one from this week, frozen treats."

"I don't know."

"That's fine. Let's see if you can find them. What are other frozen treats?"

"Ice cream."

"Yes, you have that one. What's something you add fruit into and blend it?"

"A smoothie."

"Great, that's two: ice cream and smoothie. Now, what's the last one? It comes on a stick?"

"Lollipop."

"Close, that is on a stick, but we also need it to be frozen. So what comes on a stick that's frozen?"

"Uh... Popsicle."

"Alright, so what are your three words?"

"Didn't I get all three?"

"Yes, but I want you to say all three together."

"Ice cream and smoothie."

"And one more, it's on a stick."

"Popsicle."

"Okay, now all three of your words together."

"Um... ice cream."

She will get up in the middle of the night, get fully dressed, expecting to go "home" (back to the house she lived in when she was a child), insist someone is picking her up to take her home, or just full out refuse to go back to her bedroom. Mind you, she's lived in her current house for over half a century. The speech therapist suggested we get the simple magnetic home alarms that sound when the doors are opened, just in case she tries to leave the house in the middle of the night. We've tried to get back in to see the neurologist, but they lost one of the doctors in the practice and can't get in for another four months, the appointment we made three months ago.

She has recently been following my father around more often, and it's cute to see them together. Her attitude isn't so negative with him, and I think with the diagnosis, they both understand the situation better. He helps out with her a lot, and having another person there helps lighten the load. However, as I'm still raising children, when my mother becomes more difficult to take care of, I realize I can only spread myself so thin, and when it gets too taxing, I'll be looking into a home for her.

Snippets From Others

I'm sure you've noticed that the previous stories are from children who all had a parent diagnosed with dementia. I asked several people whose significant other had the disease, and those who didn't outright tell me no didn't want to rehash the majority of those difficult memories. I don't know if I could, if I were in their shoes, but they were willing to give a little insight on a few of the struggles they faced and some tips.

You see what's happening, and you tell them to try to get out and do stuff or to play games. The kids would get us all kinds of games. They even gave us tablets and added games and books on them. But they seem like they don't even want to do anything, and looking back, you're not sure if it's because of the disease or they just didn't care and just wanted to be lazy. A few years into it, right before she was diagnosed, I calmed down about it. I guess I realized it wasn't doing any good for anyone. After the diagnosis, she settled down about it, like she'd listen and then she'd get up and exercise. The more you stay active, the better it is for everything. But when she'd go outside to walk, she wouldn't say anything, and if I came back inside or I was in another room and I didn't see her go, well, I'd worry that something might happen to her. Like her friend she had that would go driving and wind up two or three hours away. She'd get in the car, drive, and forget where she was going, give us a call, and we'd go and get her. I'm lucky my wife didn't do that; she'd just walk around the house, but there was always that worry that she'd go farther, ya know?

You want to help. You want to bring them back, so you start to try everything, but when they shoot you down, saying, "If that worked, don't you think they'd be using it in the medical field?" that gets discouraging. It's not their fault, they seem callous because it's part of the disease, but it still hurts, and that's one thing you'll have to take into consideration. No matter how much you try to do to help them, there's a good chance that part of them will fight you every step of the way.

You start out believing that, if you repeat it enough or if you write it down, he'll get it and it'll come back, but it doesn't. The hardest part is the constant "new normal" is a moving target. You'll start at one spot and get used to that, but then it changes, and it's always a loss. It's like death by a thousand cuts, slow and emotional.

Give them tasks, but easy short-direction tasks, like grab that, put this down. They still want to be useful, but they can't do much. Don't do everything for them; let them try to do it first; it'll help work what they have left.

Music is good; it uses a different part of the brain. People can oftentimes remember lyrics as opposed to anything else. You can talk to them about their favorite songs or songs of their time. Also, story telling is good for them, and exercise.

A few things that she helped me with is the realization that you need to be in the moment and enjoy the present with them. Try to meet them where they're at, find the things that can give you and them some joy. There's a sad beauty to the concept of seeing everything every day like it was the first time. The small things we take for granted, that we drive past, she'd see it and be in such awe. That's where you need to be in the present with them and embrace the beauty as they see it, and then you can share this moment with them because that moment is all they have.

Extra Tips on How to Advocate in Pursuing a Dementia Diagnosis

If the actions from the previous stories weren't enough, here is a bit of a list to help with advocating.

1) Document everything

Keep a detailed log or journal of observed changes. Use specific examples of memory lapses, confusion, personality shifts, safety issues, or difficulties with daily tasks. Make sure to include dates, frequency, and impact. This will help counter the "it's just aging" response with more compelling concrete evidence.

Here is an example:

- Monday, Jan 19th at 12:15 spent 7 minutes trying to turn on the toaster oven she has had for fifteen years. There is only one knob to turn it on.

- Monday, Jan 19th at 16:40 took 20 minutes to write a single check and in the end received help. Ended up wasting 5 checks because he couldn't place the correct items on the proper lines. This task is something he's performed for the last 50 years.

- Tuesday, Jan 20th at 17:11 while cooking dinner said that she wanted to poison her husband. Not something she has ever made a joke about or inferred for the last 52 years.

- Tuesday, Jan 20th at 18:21 cooked dinner and when it was served, the ground beef was still raw and the pasta noodles were soggy.

- Tuesday, Jan 20th at 9:45 reached into the hot frying oil to get a chicken strip and burned their hand after they had received a warning to stay clear while it was cooking.

To make things easier, in the section of this book titled "Helpful Resources" you will find a print copy and a QR code to print a blank form titled "Recorded Observed Actions" along with a couple other forms that may be of use.

2) Bring a trusted advocate to every appointment

If you've already tried to discuss the situation with your provider but nothing has changed, you may want to add a second person, whom you trust, to advocate for you. They can provide a clearer history, take notes, ask additional questions, and ensure less is overlooked.

If you're going with someone as the advocate, remember the person who asked you to go is relying on you to help get the information they need. If going with them and being persistent doesn't help, please, help them find someone who will listen. Check other primary care physicians or geriatricians.

3) Be direct and persistent, prepare questions in advance, request specific screenings

Don't wait for the doctor to suggest any test. Create a list, pull it out, and straight up ask them (politely).

For example, "I'm concerned about cognitive changes and would like to get a formal cognitive assessment such as the MoCA or the MMSE."

These are two of the typical tests, but there are others that involve detailed history and neurological exams. Make sure the person giving the test isn't handing out answers. There aren't many questions in the MoCA or the MMSE, and that may severely impact the results.

If the initial results are borderline or dismissed, remember you can always politely ask for a referral to a memory clinic or a neurologist. Although currently expensive and not widely available, there are tests such as emerging blood biomarker tests and amyloid/tau tests. Ask about specific brain imaging they could do. There are other advanced tests such as a spinal tap or the advanced cognitive testing (neuropsychological battery). Some of these tests have their own risks, so please make informed decisions.

If you haven't already asked prior to this, another question that would be good in the first appointment would be "What tests are recommended so we can rule out reversible causes?" There are several options, as stated prior, such as vitamin deficiency, depression, urinary tract infection, any side effects of currently taken medications, sleep, stress, etc.

Allow your provider the opportunity to give more options. It's likely their lack of "listening" or lack of follow-through isn't being done with malicious intent. There may be other reasons why your provider may be casting your concerns aside such as; they may not be overly experienced in dementia, they may be worried about giving a wrong diagnosis (it is called practicing medicine for a reason), or they also have severe time constraints and cannot do as thorough an assessment as they may want, to name a few.

If you're told "it's normal aging," point out that these changes are affecting daily life/safety and if your family history has dementia (blood relation), tell them.

However, no matter the reason, if they aren't giving you what you need and you've asked several times, it's more than a valid sign to look for someone who is able to get you the assistance you're requesting. It's like always going to a restaurant wanting a steak and getting soup. You don't keep going to that restaurant. It's not the restaurant's fault. They specialize in soup. It's not intentional that they aren't giving you the steak, but you need to find a new restaurant if you plan on actually getting a steak.—It's the same idea.

4) Involve other family members/loved ones strategically

If siblings or relatives notice similar issues, you can coordinate to reinforce observations, and you can share resources to build a community and consensus. Possibly have a collaboration with providers. Definitely share resources, and it'll help to know others that are traversing a similar path for all involved.

5) Additional ways to find help

US Medicare covers an annual wellness visit (including cognitive screening). You can ask then or express your concerns during that visit. They have the option to come to your home in some areas. There may be options in your region. Connect with local associations, groups, or chapters for free support, helplines, or memory clinic referrals. If you're in a rural area or a region not associated with the USA, you may need to do some digging.

Additional Tasks to Tackle While You Wait

While you're in pursuit of a diagnosis, it may seem frustratingly daunting. There are tasks that can be tackled during this time. It will not only be beneficial to complete, but also represent progress that helps alleviate some of the frustrations. By taking care of other tasks you can still be productive and you won't feel like you're just spinning your wheels. Here are some examples:

1) Legal/financial planning: Even if this has been addressed before, some may not have put too much thought into this kind of future, and it may need to be readdressed. Make sure there is a power of attorney (POA): legal, financial, medical, living will, and all that goes into that. Check with an attorney; if you cannot afford one, in most states, there is a day during the month when attorneys will provide insight on the process or possibly do it pro bono, or you can search some up in your area. Sorry, I am unaware of the estate planning process in any country besides the USA; an internet search or talking to someone in your local judicial system may be able to provide information to locate someone.

2) Advance directive: If the person with dementia has a medical POA or already addressed this with estate planning, ensure their current medical provider has a copy. If they don't have one, you should be able to ask for one from a medical provider. Fill it out and return it to them. Keeping an accessible copy close is also a beneficial idea.

3) Driving evaluations: Some go through the DMV as a request, others have an occupational therapy site where a driving simulation can be done. This isn't meant to take away the ability to drive; however, it is in the best interest of not only those in the vehicle but all people on and around the roads to ensure an accident or fatality isn't caused.

4) Home safety assessments: Do a safety walk regularly—set a certain date and time to perform this. It may not be to the point where you have to start using safety locks on specific items like you would a child (but it may be, depending on the current situation especially), but there are simple ones to keep in mind such as food safety and physical safety. For example,

- Are there chemicals, harmful materials, animals, or pests close to food, where there is a possibility that the food could become contaminated?

- Check for expired or soon-to-expire food and the condition it is being kept in to ensure it won't be consumed.

- Most typical OSHA items (it may seem extreme, but OSHA/SCATS has typical standards I am aware of, and they are easy to find/get informational material on—if these items are foreign to you, an easier place to start may be National Center for Healthy Housing see link in "Helpful Resources"), such as

    - Slip trip and fall prevention: examples of this could be cords, flooring, water, ice, debris, and other items on or around the floor. If there is any railing in the house, make sure they are intact and in good condition.

    - Electrical or heat issues that may cause fires, burns, or electrocution: examples of this would be frayed wires, poor or over-stressed sockets, debris, or flammable items too close to heat sources or items that distribute heat (like heating vents).

    - Debris or items in the way of exits or broken unused doors/windows.

    - There are several more you could look into. An easier way to think about safety is to imagine you're in a horror film and every situation may be "the scare". For example, how many people stick their hand in the garbage disposal without unplugging it? Yet when you're watching a horror film and the character does that, you think to yourself *that's such a bad idea* because YOU know they're in a horror film and anything that could cause an issue typically does.

- Do a safety walk regularly—set a certain date and time to perform this: daily/weekly/monthly. Yes, this is a repeat from before, but this is a good one to stress in any home.

5) Adopt healthier habits: You don't have to wait for a diagnosis to help delay the onset. Healthy habits such as exercise, good diet, and mental stimulation will help no matter where your loved one is. If you don't know where to start, check with a nutritionist, medical provider, physical therapist, trainer, or other professional who is knowledgeable about their current condition and able to provide valuable insight.

- Mental stimulation can be as simple as being more sociable. Getting involved in the community, volunteering, joining or signing up for a club/class/team/group, and going. Check to see if the community has senior activities or locations. Play games or puzzles such as computer, card, board, paper, or tablet/smart phone. Get your loved one to pick up a new hobby; it's a great way to make friends and be social—two birds, one stone.

- Simple game: the three words a day to remember. Pick or have someone pick three words to recall throughout the day. Another option is there are several websites that have a daily word that could be an easy substitute if you want something on your phone to remind you.

<u>6ish) Handy tips for Day-to-Day</u>: There is a chance that before you get a diagnosis or even after that these tips may come in handy for you in everyday use and hopefully help reduce hassle and stress.

- Give a 15-20 minute prep time to leave. I had to do this when I had small children because it would sometimes take a while to round them up. I realized to get to appointments on time I needed to start doing this with my mother. This would give me the buffer to make sure she went to the bathroom, got everything she needed to have and herd her into the vehicle. If you get ready to go fifteen minutes prior and then you monitor/help them it makes it so much easier.

- If you need to take them with you shopping or prefer to as it'll get them out and socializing. One item I've come to make going through stores easier is to have them "drive" the cart, and you hold on to the front steering it at a decent pace. This way you can guide them around without having to watch them like a hawk and it gives them the opportunity to feel like they're being useful. You can feel when they've let go so you're less likely to lose them. But make sure that the walking pace is easy for them to keep up with. If it's your partner and you're used to holding hands this would work as well.

- You may get to a point where going out to dinner with them isn't viable for several reasons, but you can still order out and then eat it at home. This way you get the food of eating out with less issues and less stress. Additionally, it'll be less clean-up and hassle if you're doing all of the cooking—give yourself a break especially if you can afford it. Since COVID more restaurants have a more extensive takeout menu and if you have the ability of a delivery service, that may be a good option too.

- As was stated before, give them simple (one step) tasks to help you. Make sure these tasks are okay if not done up to normal standards and make sure they have supervision so actions can be corrected, or adjusted as it's performed. Also realize, some days a simple task will be too much for them, it won't be exactly what you asked for, or they may have lost their common sense so when asking them to do something make sure to take all outcomes into consideration (literal and figurative).

- If they have a tendency to wander around and get in the way while you're trying to get things done, an easy way to curb this is to give them directions. Such as: "It's okay you can sit down." or ask them what they need or are looking for and then help them out.

- If they have an opportunity to be alone in the kitchen, bathroom or other rooms that may have personal care items or items that are used for consumption. Make sure to either hide them so they don't misuse the item, clean the item each time right before you plan to use it, or leave out mock ones to let them "use" and then get the real ones out when you need them, but do not pull them out while they are in the room. (This will help avoid odd sicknesses and additional clean up.)

These are just a few, and depending on the situation, you may need more or less.

You can find a printed copy and QR code to print out a task sheet to help you keep track of what you need as well as additional forms in the section of the book titled "Helpful Resources".

Caregivers

You do not have to do this alone. I wish someone had told me this. It would have saved a lot of stress and frustration.

Nonprofessional caregivers such as family or friends face so much stress, with impacts on mental and physical health and finances. If you are caring for a loved one or know someone who is, please make sure they are given a little respite—a few hours for a break could mean so much. In some communities, there are support groups, also adult day care or craft classes for seniors to give caregivers a break. Remember, just like in an airplane, you put your oxygen mask on first, then you will be better able to help others.

Aside from the safety setup from earlier, especially if you will be doing a good amount of the caregiving, here are some things that may be helpful:

1)<u>Child safety locks on items that may lead to hazards</u>, such as

- Doors and gates that lead to busy streets or outside

- Cabinets that house chemicals

- Oven, stove, and other heat-producing appliances

2)**If there's a microwave, foil and other metal items need to be removed** because there is a chance they'll put it in the microwave. Or remove the microwave altogether.

3)**If they have a pet, limit the amount of critter treats they have access to and items that, if the animal consumes, could make them sick**, such as chocolate for most animals and loose medication.

4) **Limit sweets as well as sugary drinks**. Many people with dementia crave sweets.

- Always keep easily accessible fruit for when they want something sweet and easily accessible healthy treats.

- Ask friends and family members not to give boxes of chocolates or junk food directly to them. Chances are they will eat the entire amount within a few hours and could make themselves sick. It may sound a little ridiculous, but there will be a point when you'll need to ration treats, or they will consume them all and possibly make themselves sick.

5)**Use small electric appliances with automatic shut-off switches** such as a kettle or any others that are used regularly.

6)Remove the step stools and move wanted/needed items within reach to help prevent falls and falling items. If you are worried about them having certain items, remove them completely (many times it is out of sight, out of mind).

7)Keep disposable gloves on hand for extra messes in several areas, especially the bathroom.

8)For convenience, slowly replace clothing with elasticized trousers or other easy-assist clothes and front-clasping velcro bras. There are good cotton arthritis bras that need not be removed for X-rays. Shoes should be easy on and off as well, but not where they come off as they're walking.

9)Be aware when they start using adult incontinence pants that you may need to regularly check the dresser drawers and dirty clothes hamper for soiled garments that were "put away" to use again or wash.

10)Place large time pieces in a prominent location.

- Digital clock showing day of the week and AM and PM time
- Keep a calendar with large squares where you can write down everything on their schedule, such as what time medical appointments are, when they go to church each week, visits with friends, and any other activities that are happening.

11)Have all important phone numbers laminated and kept in several places. Although, if the constant ringing of the phone is an issue or they become more frustrated with trying to answer or make calls or cannot make calls, you may want to weigh whether keeping their personal cell phone is in their best interest.

12)Label items for simplicity (If you are familiar with the 5S workplace organization, this would help a bunch).

- Moisturizers, day (especially if it has SPF) and night
- Appliances, such as the freezer and the refrigerator
- Remote controls, if you can get simple ones, it's best, and label what they go to
- Other often-used items that get confused with others

13)With so much to manage, if you keep everything as simple as possible, it will make things less stressful in a stress-filled situation.

There may be several local groups that can give assistance. Ask your provider, a senior center, local church, or county or city public office. Many local churches may do Meals on Wheels. There are adult day cares, but check to see if they can leave on their own accord. There are organizations that can come to the house and take care of your loved one while you can get a break, run errands, etc. Taking care of a loved one with dementia is taxing, no matter how much you love them, and it is MORE than okay to get some respite.

Each caregiver in the stories above all had a set limit to when they were going to let someone else help carry the load of their loved one's care. If you need to tap out, that is more than understandable. It bears repeating that you should not feel guilty once you've made a decision regarding either being a caregiver or finding a home for your loved one. Just a reminder of the importance of having your family member appoint you as their POA, as well as their medical appointee, before they become mentally unable to make these decisions.

When Looking for a Care Home

In the USA, if you haven't gotten a medical POA or an ROI (release of information), make sure you have one before you place someone in a home, or you'll struggle getting your loved one's information due to the HIPPA act. I can only assume elsewhere this may be a problem as well, so you may need to do a local search for release of information for elderly patients in memory care. A local ombudsman may be able to help you find some locations to look into. An ombudsman is a person who typically advocates for elders in care homes, as well as other items, so check your local area to see if your local ombudsman is able to assist you.

Memory care facilities specialize in seniors with different forms of dementia. If there is one close, it may be a good option. We'd still suggest asking questions, as not all facilities are created equal. However, most of these will have the facility locked and only allow certain registered family members in there because they are trying to prevent unauthorized people from getting in to take advantage of the vulnerable residents. This kind of care typically includes the following:

- Specialized environment and a secured facility to prevent wandering
- Designed spaces to help reduce stress and anxiety
- Staff-provided tailored care and activities, including physical, occupational and speech therapies along with music and art therapy

There are several different types and sizes of homes. Some of these tips will likely apply to larger or different types of homes as well, but I went with the smaller locations. The first questions you can get away with asking over the phone to save time, and if they pass that test, you can go for the in-person interview. Some of the questions will be answered correctly over the phone but in practice may not be the same. Being told things are a certain way as opposed to actually witnessing them makes a difference. I learned this the hard way. Sometimes the homes aren't trying to hide anything; they just don't think it's important, especially if you don't ask. You can find a printed copy and QR code to a form to print out with these questions in the chapter titled "Helpful Resources".

Phone questions

- What is the staff to resident ratio?
- Is the facility alarmed or locked at every exit?

- Is someone awake during the night or only sleeping on site? (Many residents get up or will try to at night. If this is a concern, it will be important to have an awake person at night to avoid falls or other issues. Especially if they typically need assistance to walk but may forget they need help.)

- How and where are the meals distributed? Is it in their room? Is it everyone eating together, like a family?

- What kind of meals are prepared?

- Are the other residents verbal? (If your loved one is still able to communicate, you'll want to make sure they can get needed stimulation and conversation, and not just from the busy staff.)

In-person questions and items to ensure/observe are there

- Is the main door alarmed or locked? (Elderly people easily wander off, so having a door chime is an extra precaution.)

- Just inside the door, there should be a place to sign in and out, health certificates and licenses should be prominently displayed, and hand sanitizer, and masks offered.

- Take in the smell. There might be the occasional unpleasant aroma, but overall, does it smell like it is cleaned regularly and cleaned well?

- Does the home look clean? Look at the communal areas, kitchen, bathrooms, bedrooms, floors, etc.
- Is the furniture shabby? Old, perfectly functioning furniture is fine. (The other side of this coin is... is the furniture super new and flashy? Is more care being put into appearances than comfort and care?)
- Are fresh fruit and healthy snacks available for the residents on the kitchen counter?
- Is there an area where residents can be together, reading, doing puzzles, or watching television? (Just a comfortable place so they don't feel lonely.)
- Is there a place for visitors to comfortably sit?
- If at all possible, visit during meal times or in the morning. (Visiting in the afternoon is often nap time and you won't be able to see the place when it is alive.)
- How do the residents look? Are they well tended to? (Chat with them. These will be the people your loved one is living with, and many of them are so sweet. Even if they are confused, their personality often shines

through.)

- Are there cameras in the home? (This may or may not be important to you.)
- If you can get a contract before, or have time to read it over, do so. Highlight or add sticky notes with questions and get clarification. It's okay to set it up like you're taking a test—your loved one depends on it.

Extra Insight from Ruby's Daughter Regarding Care Homes

She says, "Trust your gut. I think I could walk into a board and care home now and easily spot the fraudsters out to make money over the genuinely caring folks. This, sadly, wasn't always the case."

The contracts I saw required a thirty-day written notice to move the resident out. The only exception being if they die. In this case, you should be entitled to money for the days they did not use that month, as long **as you remove every single item of theirs from the premises**. It's grueling to go in the day after your loved one has passed, but I'd advise doing it if you are able to. I took three bags: one for items to keep, one to give away, and one for trash. If you cannot do it, ask someone else to assist and just gather everything up for you until you can go through it. If you had a hospital device delivered to the location, or a wheelchair, it is your responsibility to contact the company and tell them these items need collecting as soon as possible. Keeping the home informed meant they did not charge me for the days we waited for the collection of said items. It also meant we were not charged for the items. This is something easily overlooked while dealing with the other mountain of things one needs to tend to when a loved one passes.

When you have signed a contract and placed your loved one in a home but realize they are being neglected and not getting the care promised, they are *not* stuck in that home. It can feel overwhelming to think you must find another home and move them yet again, but it will be a relief once you have done so. I am not saying this will work for you, but the way I got out of the contract was this: I wrote a letter outlining everywhere the home was failing in care, including having one staff member on for seven weeks, 24/7, without a break to care for five residents, serving only frozen food, with absolutely nothing fresh, and regularly running out of toilet paper. My letter stated the day I would move my mother out and that I would be paying ONLY for the days she was in residence. I let the owner know that I had contacted the ombudsman for elder care, alerted them to the failings of the home, and gave them a copy of the letter as well.

The ombudsman, aware of my plans, made a case number, visited the home, and interviewed residents and visiting family members. Their visit, along with my letter to the owner, meant I was able to move my mother out with very little drama. On the day I was packing up Mom's belongings to move her, the owner turned up and tried to talk me into staying, putting on her sweetest voice, making excuses, etc... but I very calmly told her we were leaving, as nothing she promised was reality.

I tell you all of this not to discourage you but to empower you. Even when trying to find the best fit, it doesn't always work out. Don't ever give up, and look for services who can assist you. Sadly, if I hadn't been visiting my mother most days,

I wouldn't have known how awful the home was. If you don't live nearby, try to arrange to have a friend or family visit on different days. One home required visitors to phone ahead to see if it was a convenient time to visit. I'm not sure I liked that idea, as if they might be trying to hide something or "prepare" your loved one somehow. I'm sure they had their reasons, but that didn't sit well with us. There are many wonderful homes out there, but there are also some pretty bad ones. Elder care is an enormous money-making business. Sadly, some facilities and owners place greed over actual care."

Helpful Resources

We are not affiliated with any of the links below; however, these are a few that were suggested to one of the people in this book or they were used for extra research. There are a myriad of options, materials, books, and activities out there, that may be good as well (as stated before this is not a comprehensive list). Although, these can be a decent starting point for those who aren't sure where to start or where to go next. Additional resources are available in a search or you can ask for additional resources from your provider, local senior citizens community, or local church.

LINKS

https://alz-journals.onlinelibrary.wiley.com/doi/10.1002/alz.70235

https://www.alz.org/alzheimers-dementia/facts-figures

https://www.alz.org/help-support/resources

https://www.alzdiscovery.org/cognitive-vitality/blog/targeting-14-lifestyle-factors-may-prevent-up-to-45-of-dementia-cases

https://consultqd.clevelandclinic.org/the-difficult-essential-talk-about-dementia

https://conversationstoremember.org/geriatricians-who-they-are-why-they-are-important-and-why-we-need-more/

https://deerprogram.org/dementia-self-management/

https://www.forbes.com/sites/howardgleckman/2026/01/26/as-numbers-of-older-adults-grow-the-supply-of-doctors-isnt-keeping-up/

https://journals.lww.com/mjdy/fulltext/2025/09000/the_new_type_3_diabetes_mellitus__a_growing.2.aspx

https://pmc.ncbi.nlm.nih.gov/articles/PMC12206097/

https://mariashriver.com/alzheimers/

https://www.powershealth.org/about-us/newsroom/health-library/2025/01/21/most-dementia-patients-unaware-of-diagnosis

https://nchh.org/resources/standards-and-assessments/checklists/

https://www.yalemedicine.org/news/7-strategies-to-lower-your-risk-for-dementia

https://youtube.com/shorts/eyuHSQXVtoY?is=L1dHsKHFh_FDQnzA

FORMS

You can copy them off and use or they have been set up to be pulled out if wanted instead.

Recorded Observed Actions

#	Day	Date:	Time	Item observed	Why it's concerning.
1					

Tasks to Tackle While You Wait

You can take the list from the chapter "Additional Tasks to Tackle While You Wait" and insert what you need to take care of below. You can check them off and add a few others you need or pick and choose everything you'd like on it.

Tasks to Tackle

✓	Date	Task	Follow up items / New appointments / Numbers
☐			
☐			
☐			
☐			
☐			
☐			
☐			
☐			
☐			
☐			
☐			
☐			
☐			
☐			
☐			
☐			
☐			
☐			
☐			
☐			
☐			
☐			

Questions for a Care Home

Open spaces have been provided so you can write down any additional questions you may have.

	Name of Home:						
	Question:	Y/N	Home 1 Extra notes	Y/N	Home 2 Extra notes	Y/N	Home 3 Extra notes
OVER THE PHONE	What is the staff to resident ratio?						
	Is the facility alarmed or locked at every exit?						
	Is someone awake during the night or only sleeping on site?						
	How and where are the meals distributed? Is it in their room? Is it everyone eating together, like a family?						
	What kind of meals are prepared?						
	Are the other residents verbal?						
IN-PERSON QUESTIONS AND ITEMS TO ENSURE/OBSERVE	Is the main door alarmed or locked?						
	Just inside the door, there should be a place to sign in and out, health certificates and licenses displayed, hand sanitizer and masks offered?						
	Take in the smell. Does it smell like it is cleaned regularly and cleaned well?						
	Does the home look clean? Kitchen Bathrooms, bedrooms, floors, etc.						
	Is the furniture shabby? Old, perfectly functioning furniture or is it super new and flashy?						
	Is more care being put into trying to keep up appearances than comfort and care?						
	Are fresh fruit and healthy snacks available for the residents on the kitchen counter or in an easily accessible location?						
	Is there an area where residents can be together reading, doing puzzles, or watching television?						
	Is there a place for visitors to comfortably sit?						
	Where you able to witness the home during a meal? How was the food? How was the atmospshere? Where did they all eat?						
	How do the residents look? Are they well tended to? Were they willing to chat?						
	Are there cameras in the home? Where are they at? How many are there?						

QR CODE for the previous forms

Afterword

This book is not meant to be used as medical advice or to replace any medical advice given by medical professionals. The opinions offered are just that, opinions from people with no claim to medical knowledge, just experience in life.

We hope this book was of some help at getting you to move on to the next stage that you're looking to. Without sounding too much like a broken record: educate, advocate, educate, advocate, until you get to where you need to be. Hopefully, this little insight into our personal journeys will help you find the best way for you and your loved one. We wish you nothing but the best. Remember to laugh. Even in the cruelty and despair of dementia, some things are funny. Keeping a sense of humor truly helped in our situations, for our loved ones and us.

We wish you luck on this journey.

About the Authors

Rhys Shaw and V.V. Marie both live on the West Coast of the United States. Between them, they have over ten published fiction books but felt it was important to put their skills into a topic that has impacted them both. With this book *A Fight To Find An Answer*, both V.V. Marie and Rhys Shaw hope to share their experiences with those who may need the same help in traversing the murky waters that are all too familiar when advocating for someone with dementia.

www.ingramcontent.com/pod-product-compliance
Lightning Source LLC
LaVergne TN
LVHW060453061126
851857LV00016B/1812
9781970758016